THE ART OF RUSSIA

THE ART OF
RUSSIA

BY

HELEN RUBISSOW

PHILOSOPHICAL LIBRARY

NEW YORK · 1946

THE LIBRARY
COLBY JUNIOR COLLEGE
NEW LONDON, N. H.

ND
681
R8

COPYRIGHT, 1946, BY

THE PHILOSOPHICAL LIBRARY, INC.

15 EAST 40TH STREET, NEW YORK, N. Y.

27704

EAST AND WEST

Between the two sources of culture— the East and the West—Russia appears to be not so much a barrier, as the meeting ground. Since olden days, cultural values flowed towards her towns, which united and assimilated the most varied trends, and thence spread them once more with the four winds, all over Russia's wide expanse. Thus, in

Russian folk ornament which embellishes everything from the embroidered collar of a shirt to the honey-bun and a temple cornice, it is easy to trace the Scandinavian, Persian and Indian motives. The reindeer of the North, the rooster and the swan, meet with the Persian lion and the peacock; and the modest northern daisies and cranberries mingle with luxuriant flowers of Indian origin. Such ornamentation also shows clearly the influence of the Scythians, the ancient inhabitants of southern Russia. Even more obvious in it is the Mongolian heritage. In the 13th century, the Tatar hordes of Ghenghis Khan and Batu overran Russia, in huge Oriental waves. The Tatar yoke lasted for two and a half centuries, during which time Russia was separated from the family of European nations and held from all participation in the artistic development of the "Great European School."

ICON

Through Kiev—"The Mother of Russian cities"—the Byzantine influence had penetrated into Russia in the tenth century, along with Christianity. The Church brought the icon and with it the art of painting.

In the workshops of monasteries the first Russian painters, the monks, learned the art of easel and mural painting in order to beautify their temples. Their teachers were Greek painters. Among the latter, a master by the name of Theophanos, nicknamed "the philosopher," who came to Russia toward the end of the 14th century, was distinguished by originality and forceful talent. Theophanos left remarkable examples of mural painting in the temples and private houses of Novgorod and Moscow. These

two cities for a number of centuries remained genuine centers of painting.

Among the pupils of Theophanos was a young monk from a monastery near Moscow, Andrew Rublev, who became the greatest Russian painter of icons. Like Giotto in Italy, Rublev infused the traditional religious art of Byzantine with a new content. The composition of his icons reflects a new kind of rhythm, not frozen in cold monumentality, but fluent; while their colors are softer and warmer. Of Rublev's icons, the best known is *The Trinity*, (see illustrations, plate 3) now in the Tretyakov State Gallery in Moscow.

Another great icon painter was Dionysius, of the late 15th and early 16th century. His icons are remarkable for their colouring; they seem to be transfused with golden light, transforming everything material and making the icon, according to the description of A. Avinoff, a "reflection of spiritual otherworldliness." * In their composition they show great independence although, as in the icons of Rublev, the purity of the Byzantine tradition is fully sustained. Avinoff writes of this remarkable master: "In the fanciful backgrounds of Dionysius, . . . in the extreme, elongated stylizing of his figures, we may see a counterpart to many startling effects of so-called modernists. Matisse and Modigliani would, probably, look at him with approbation."

At the end of the 16th century, the increased influence of the East was strongly reflected in the icons of the so-called "Stroganov School" (Plate 6), which was named in honor of its patrons, the Stroganovs, an influential and wealthy family of merchants. They were great connoisseurs of the art of the East, of Persian miniatures, of Indian textiles and jewelry, as well as of the icon, in which they appreciated the rich Oriental display of colors and ornamentation. The Stroganov School thrived through the years of this family's flourishing, and drooped to its decadence with the Stroganovs' fall, in the early 17th century.

The leading role in icon-painting then passed to the so-called "Tsar's painters," who were organized by the Tsarist government into a special atelier related to the State Armoury. Among the members of this atelier were several former Stroganov painters. A number of names have reached us from this period: Emelian Moscovitin, Prokofyi

* A. Avinoff. Russian Icons. Collection of George R. Hahn, Carnegie Institute, Pittsburgh, 1944.

Shchirin, Nikifor, Nazary Savin (Plate 7). Although in the works of art of the Tsar's painters, the old mysticism still survived, a leaning towards greater realism can be observed at times; for instance, in the treatment of faces and figures, as well as in the introduction of a more elaborate landscape. The sharp and bare Byzantine rocks are occasionally covered with woods or replaced by fields; and from somewhere, out of the unknown, outer world, a serpentine path leads to the church. At this period, however, signs of decline become apparent—such as the overburdening of the design with decorations and details, to the detriment of the whole. This is manifest in the icons painted by "Friaz." * Friaz is an artistic manner representing the mixture of the last echo of the Byzantine religious art with new influences that penetrated from the West. Representatives of this painting were  S. Ushakov, J. Kazanetz, and G. Kondratiev, who often worked collectively on the same icon, V. Poznansky, and others. The icons of such painters, despite their color effects and great professional skill, present all the signs of the passing away of the great ancient art that generally precede the birth of the new.

This "new" art was driving from the West: "worldly" art, individual art, colored by the personal emotions and thoughts of the artist—in a word, painting in the European sense. It began in Russia at the end of the 17th century, during the reign of the Emperor Peter the Great, when Russian history, and with it art, "turned towards the West." Under Peter, there came to Russia, a land newly discovered by European society, foreign painters who brought with them secular subjects and artistic skill. At the same time, the Boyars (great landowners) began to send their most talented dependents to the West, to study the art of reproducing objects.

THE 18TH CENTURY

The first art school was established in St. Petersburg, and canvases by Russian painters began to appear. Following the tradition of their foreign masters, the Russian painters of the time reflected in their work the subject that dominated the contemporary art of western Europe, namely, court life. In the 18th century, particularly during the reign of Peter the Great's daughter, Elizabeth, court life in Russia attained great brilliance. The painter of the time was required to produce chiefly decorative, alle-

* Friaz—from the word "Frank" or "French"; generally an icon of free interpretation, in which the influence of the European, particularly German, worldly art is strongly felt. For the Russian poorly educated man of the peasant masses, the words "German" and "French" were almost synonymous, meaning "foreign."

gorical panels, glorifying the activities of various highly-placed personages, as well as portraits of these personages and their relatives.

In consequence, there appeared among the painters many skilful portraitists, whose work was often in no measure inferior in talent and technique to that of their colleagues in western Europe. Such are some of the portraits by A. Antropov (Plate 10), I. Argunov, G. Ugryumov (Plate 11), F. Rokotov (Plate 13), D. Levitzky (Plate 14), V. Borovikovsky (Plate 15). Particularly well known are Levitzky and Borovikovsky, partly, however, because of the greater quantity of their paintings.

In spite of the fact that most of the painters of that group had risen from the people, their art scarcely touched upon the folk life—which, together with the country's physical aspects, represents the chief source of the autochthonous in art. But the people found a characteristic means of self-expression, in the movement of Russia toward the family of western European nations. At the end of the 17th century, there began to appear popular Russian pictures known under the general term of *lubok,* that is, print (originally woodcut).* In them, lush ornament is combined with representations of incidents

from the lives of the people. The *lubok* (Plates 8, 9) represents a complex phenomenon, and a whole literature has developed around it. The best known and the most complete work on the subject is in the five volumes of D. A. Rovinsky's *Russian Popular Pictures.*

The *lubok* came into existence chiefly by way of imitation, by the Russian self-taught masters, of the many engravings imported from western Europe. But the best of those pictures are no longer imitations, they directly reflect the original life of the people, and are very rich in content. Here we find the Russian landscape and scenes from everyday life represented either with naive humor or biting satire; everything, in short, that was allowed no access to the "great art" of the court, or, later, of the Academy.

Another channel through which the original popular art manifested itself was the miniature. We find abundant samples of this in old books. For the most part, those books are religious in content, but in the illustrations drawn by the monks there often appear scenes from ordinary life. A good example of a book of this type is the manuscript, *Medicine for the Soul,* which was kept in the Hall of Arms in Moscow. Its excellent miniatures were executed by the monks of the Troitse-

* "Lubok" from "lub", bast, inner bark, which was originally used in the fabrication of a cheap cliché for a print.

Sergievsky (the Trinity and St. Sergius) Monastery, headed by N. Kuzmin, in the year 1670.

Remarkable miniaturists were the *Paleshane*,* mentioned for the first time in the archives in the 17th century. Since remote times, the inhabitants of the villages Palekh, Kholui and Mstery in the Province of Vladimir, had devoted themselves to the painting of icons. History has not preserved the names of the first Paleshane icon painters; but one may safely say that they knew to perfection the technique of their art. Their customers were chiefly clerics and wealthy merchants, who liked good icons and paid well for them. With the introduction of printing, the Paleshane found themselves confronted with a new type of competition, the cheap religious prints issued in large quantities for the masses. These flooded the market, competing strongly with icons.

The village of Palekh, which produced the best and most expensive icons, suffered comparatively little from that competition, because its market continued to exist. Moreover, the Paleshane found a new use for their art. They began to produce lacquered boxes of papier maché. The miniatures that embellished those boxes, used for powder, pencils and other purposes, are true works of art. In them purity of color, understanding of composition, rhythmical quality, and firmness of design, all inherited from the masters of Byzantium, combine with a wealth of ornamentation and masterful lacquering equal in quality to the Persian and Chinese. In the subjects of the Paleshane miniatures, the themes of icons became combined with those of folklore: saints, flowers, demons, beasts and human beings are fantastically interwoven in bright but at the same time strictly formal compositions.

That peculiar village-academy, with the by-laws and discipline of an Order, although the revolution of 1917 wrought great changes in its life and work, exists to this day.

In 1748, in the reign of Empress Elizabeth, the Academy of Art was founded in St. Petersburg (now Leningrad). It developed out of the nucleus of the Department of Representative Arts of the Academy of Science, which had existed since the days of Catherine I. In 1757, the Academy of Art was reorganized by I. Shuvalov, an excellent administrator and a fine connoisseur of art.

CLASSICISM

The St. Petersburg Academy of Art followed the tradition of all academies by becoming the seat of doctrine, of imposed rules and laws. At the end of the 18th cen-

* Palekh artists.

tury and the beginning of the 19th, the doctrine it upheld was neo-classicism (pseudo-classicism). Neo-classicism was a relic of the Renaissance which, by the middle of the 18th century, had degenerated into an effete, elaborate baroque.

The excavation of Herculaneum (1738) and of Pompeii (1748) brought to light new examples of the harmonious Graeco-Roman art, and influenced modern art to assume a character of actuality. Painters once again began to turn for inspiration to history and the mythology of ancient Greece and Rome. Neo-classicism thus became the official trend of the St. Petersburg Academy of Art. A. Losenko, one of the professors who enjoyed great popularity (his painting, *Hector and Andromache*, can well serve as an example of the pseudo-classical style), produced "the canon of ideal proportions of the human body." The Academy also made mythological subjects obligatory. Losenko; Kozlov; Akimov (Plate 12); Ugryumov and his pupils, Egorov and Shebuyev, all produced paintings on mythological subjects.

But by the middle of the 18th century there were already appearing paintings on subjects of everyday life, such, for instance, as *The Young Painter* by I. Firsov and *The*

Betrothal (Plate 17) by Shibanov. These two paintings show the influence of the Dutch, with their realism and mastery of lights and shadows. In the painting by Firsov (which for some time was attributed to Losenko) the whole canvas is flooded with a mellow sunlight, which infuses the objects and people with a peculiar kind of nobility, warmth, and life. Shibanov's painting, marked with the year 1777, aside from a craftsmanship rare in those days, is remarkable because of its mighty striving towards truthfulness and its psychological approach; the faces of the bridegroom and bride are astonishingly expressive, while the types of persons that surround them are original and evidently painted mainly from life. Russia's countryside and people are depicted also in the paintings of Martynov, Galaktionov, the landscapes of F. Alexeiev (*The Neva Quai* and others) (Plate 16), *The Village Fair* and *The Troika* by Tankov.

ROMANTICISM

At the beginning of the 19th century, European art—and with it Russian art—changed from classicism to romanticism. With the development and growth of the painters' individualities, the framework of classicism, with its brilliant but cold and alien patterns, became too narrow. Art rejected them and returned to the complex world of the nuances of human experience. Olympian calm was replaced by romantic storm. The portrait ceased to be official and "magnificent"; it became warmer and more expressive.

This change is reflected in the portraits by O. Kiprensky (Plate 20), and V. Tropinin (Plates 21, 22), in the first half of the 19th century.

In the middle of the 19th century, a considerable contribution to Russian art was made by the two important painters, K. Bryullov (Plate 23) and F. Bruni. Their monumental canvases combine the traditions of classicism and romanticism, although they perhaps appear cold and over-formal to the modern eye accustomed to an entirely new artistic approach. Bryullov's *The Last Day of Pompeii* (Plate 24) amazes by its academic mastery, but does not touch the heart. Much closer to us are his smaller works, such as the Italian sketches and paintings: for instance, his delightful *Italian Girl*, flooded with joyful sunlight, or the Byronic *Turkish Woman* (Plate 25).

Bruni (Plates 26, 27) (*The Brass Serpent* is his major work), a contemporary, follower, and rival of Bryullov, is drier, darker, and more sparing of color. He is not alien to the Byzantine tradition, and in the last years of his life took to painting icons.

Bryullov and Bruni had many followers and pupils. Among the latter were Prince Gagarin (Plate 19), von Moller (Plate 18), Tyranov. To the same school belong K. Flavitzky (Plate 28) (his painting, *Princess Tarakanova*, is widely known), and the somewhat later painters, Semiradsky, Yakoby, and Polenov.

The work of one of the greatest Russian painters, A. Ivanov (Plates 29, 30, 31), touches upon the romantic school. He spent twenty-five years of his life in Italy, whither he had been sent by the Society for the Encouragement of the Arts. In the art of the Italian Renaissance the enthusiasm for ancient Greece and Rome was combined with a strong religious tendency. The tender Madonnas of Raphael, the titanic saints of Michael Angelo, like the Russian icons, must count among their ancestors the saint-images of Byzantium. In the art of the 19th century, this tendency manifested itself in the school of "Nazarenes," founded in Rome by a group of Viennese painters with Overbeck at their head. Ivanov met these artists in Rome and their influence upon his art was quite pronounced.

Ivanov's art is deeply religious, but contains at the same time traits of realism; in his presentation, the life of Christ appears a vivid reality. His technical knowledge is very great, but he is free from the coldness of the monumentally decorative style that marks the works of Bryulov and Bruni. Ivanov's seriousness and devotion to his art can well be judged by the fact that his painting *The Appearance of Christ before the People* took thirty years to paint.

Ivanov's pupil and follower, N. Gay, is closer to the realistic than to the romantic school. He depicts reality somewhat crudely, without romantic beautifying, approaching the bareness of the symbol, as in his *Golgotha* (Plates 32, 33). Something in his work appears to bring him closer, not to tender Italy, but to tragic Spain, the land of contrasts and conflicts. An inner conflict, a clash between two worlds, two wills, two opposite ideologies, is the theme of *Peter and Alexis* (Plate 34). The qualities of a psychologist are revealed also in Gay's excellent portraits, painted with great artistic craftsmanship. Such are the portraits of Tolstoy, Herzen and Mrs. Petrunkevich.

The striving towards realism became stronger and more intense in Russia, as in western Europe, in the middle of the 19th century. Tired of roaming through romantic fogs, the painters began to seek—and find—sources of inspiration in the natural environment.

To reflect life, to study nature, was the purpose of A. Venetzianov (Plates 41, 42), a pupil of Borovikovsky. Not satisfied with the academic policy, he founded his own school outside the Academy's walls. Among his pupils were Krylov, Tyranov, Shedrovsky, and Zarianko. Venetzianov's art is based on an attentive and loving study of Russian nature and the life of the Russian people. Nonetheless, he pays measure of tribute to his epoch in his partial failure to avoid sentimental idealization. In the later generation of realists, a similar place is held by K. Makovsky (Plates 51, 52).

REALISM OF GENRE AND PURPOSE

A painter of customs in the full sense of the word was P. Fedotov. He thoroughly knew the life of the middle class to which he belonged, and he depicted its humorous and its weak aspects. But his paintings are good-natured. In *The Major comes to woo* (Plate 45) the maiden is touching in her timidity; and even *The New Cavalier*—a small bureaucrat who had just received a decoration and is puffed up with pride—is not without the peculiar pathos of an actor who, barefoot, clad in a dressing gown, sincerely plays on an untidy stage the role of a "brilliant cavalier." In *The Little Widow* (Plate 44), there is much tenderness and true feeling.

By contrast, V. Perov, advancing further in the development of the social theme, sharpened the painting of customs into keen satire. With the development of the materialistic philosophy and the birth of a revolutionary movement in Russia, the social theme acquired an especial timeliness. Perov devoted himself to the castigation of the vices of the power-holding classes—the merchants and bureaucrats, as well as the clergy. Characteristic are such paintings as *The Arrival of the Governess* (Plate 46), *The Tea*, and *The Policeman*. In other pictures, such as *A Peasant's Funeral*, Perov presents the hard life of the luckless peasantry. He possessed a keen power of observation, both psychological and artistic. This is particularly apparent in his portraits (as, for instance, those of Ostrovsky and Dostoievsky) (Plate 48). Undetracted by denunciation and sermon, he allows free scope in these, to the qualities of a draftsman and a colorist.

Because the Moscow School of Painting and Sculpture was much freer from tradition than the Academy of St. Petersburg, Moscow became the center of the realistic school. There, new ideas in art were freely accepted, and encouraged.

Following in Perov's footsteps, his pupils and followers painted almost exclusively social themes. The best among them, such as N. Bogdanov-Belsky, I. Pryanishnikov (Plate 49), N. Yaroshenko (Plates 53, 54), or V. Makovsky (Plate 60), still preserved to some degree the discipline of a school, with rather strong composition and design and attentiveness to the model. But the theme kept gaining in importance, to the detriment of the artistic form. The composition and draftsmanship of many painters of that group are flabby and trite.

An independent position between the academicians and the realists is occupied by G. Semiradsky (Plate 40) and V. Polenov (Plates 38, 39). Polenov, who in essence closely approaches the school of Ivanov and Gay, was also a master of landscape and an excellent colorist. Semiradsky learned to combine traditional academic composition with the color aspirations of the impressionists, thus infusing his work with life and brilliance. A good example of his art is *Frina* (Plate 40), highly festive, despite the academic treatment of the subject.

The Academy did not follow the spirit of the times; it continued as of old to force its pupils to paint mythological and allegorical themes. Many resisted, and an opposition group was formed under the leadership of Kramskoy who, while remaining a pupil and follower of A. Ivanov, inclined rather towards the "genre realism." But in his works, such as *The Portrait of an Unknown Lady* (Plate 36) and *The Portrait of Tolstoy* (Plate 37), there is that balance between content and form which always marks the true artist.

In 1863 a protest that was almost a revolution took place in the Academy. Thirteen pupils, all candidates for the gold medal, refused to present examination works on the obligatory mythological subject; they left the Academy and formed "The Artists' Guild." A few years later, this became the nucleus of The Society of Itinerant Exhibitions ("The Wanderers").

The trend of "story" and "purpose" painting reached its apogee in the "Itinerants." To this group belonged many important painters, such as I. Repin and I. Levitan.

Repin enjoys great esteem in present-day Russia. A. Lebedev, in one of his popular books in "The Library of the Masses," writes:

"Repin's art represents that vivifying source which also feeds Soviet art."

Repin (Plate 61) treats social subjects with great artistic expressiveness and originality. *The Haulers*, one of his earlier paintings, remains also one of his most powerful. So far as composition is concerned, it is one of the best products of the Russian school. In *The Zaporozhtsy* (Ukrainian Cossacks) (Plate 62) Repin displays a great talent for color, as well as knowledge of Cossack life, with which he had been familiar since childhood. The painting represents an episode from the unruly, daring Cossack past.

Church Procession (Plate 63) is dynamic and colorful, while its idea represents a complex psychological study. In *Ivan the Terrible* (Plate 65) the psychological interest reaches its zenith. The painting almost repels with the force of its grief and horror. It is no wonder that an "attempt" was made on the painting: in 1913, a madman slashed it with a knife. (Thanks to skilful restoration, the cuts cannot be seen.)

Two other great painters of the realistic school, V. Vereshchiagin and V. Surikov, drew their subjects from Russian history.

Vereshchiagin (Plate 55) is often called a painter of battles. This is not quite correct, because the traditional painter of battles usually finds an attractive force in the battles themselves and art of this kind represents a peculiar idealization of war (a phenomenon perhaps unavoidable, but nonetheless frightening). But Vereshchiagin presents the sorrow of war. *Requiem* shows, in a tragic wilderness, rows of dead, like the beds of some horrible garden; a priest with a thurible celebrates the funeral rite in the presence of a single man, who has bared his head in memory of his fallen comrades. There is an even greater dread in the painting *All Quiet on the Shipka*, while the pyramid of skulls in *The Apotheosis of War* (Plate 56) is a symbol of the horror of war terrifying in its bareness. On the frame of that painting, the painter wrote the dedication:

"To all great conquerors of the present, the past, and the future."

Surikov (Plates 66, 67) was a man of entirely different cast of mind. He approached a painting, first of all, as a picture—not as an idea. The idea is born of itself from the pictures of life. The painter and art-critic Golovin,* writes, quoting Surikov's own words, that the idea for his painting, *The Morning of the Execution of the Streltzy*, was born in his mind because of the reflection of a candle's light on a white shirt; while "the impetus for the creation of the painting *Boyarinia Morozova* (Plate 66) was given by a black crow on white snow." Both paintings are among Surikov's best. His manner is original. The dynamism of his creation is revealed also in the use of color. In spite of a careless, occasionally dull blackness, the master's gift produces new harmonious combinations and unexpected effects. Surikov's influence upon his contemporaries was great.

Side by side with historic and genre painting, there developed also landscape painting. From the epoch of classicism there remain the Italian landscapes of Sylvester Schiedrin and M. Lebedev. Italy exerted a great attraction upon the Russian eye and heart; it served as a symbol of happy, sunlit brilliance. The famous Russian marine painter, I. Aivazovsky, who was in love with the waves of all the seas, also paid tribute to Italy.

But as classicism retreated before realism, the interest in Russian nature grew stronger. F. Vassiliev, who unfortunately died while still very young, left several paint-

* A. Golovin "Encounters and Impressions." Printed by "Iskusstvo," 1940, Leningrad-Moscow.

ings that depict the peculiar, melancholy charm of nature in a Russian village. I. Shishkin (Plates 58, 59), who knew as none other the life of the Russian forest, was an excellent draftsman. His painting is somewhat dry, but his genuine love of his subject infuses his work with life.

A search for the purity of color and new light effects, and a striving towards simpler design mark the painting of A. Kuindzhi (Plate 71). In Russia, he was one of the popularizers of impressionism and greatly influenced the Russian landscape painters of the end of the 19th and the beginning of the 20th centuries: Rylov, (Plate 131), Bogayevsky (Plate 132), Gaush, and others.

In 1817 appeared the painting by A. Savrasov, *The Rooks Have Come* (Plate 57). It proved epoch-making in the history of Russian landscape paintings. The picture amazingly conveys the elusive charm of the slow, solemn Russian spring. A plain covered with thawing snow, a belfry of an ancient church, a few slender birches around which dash in a joyful circle the birds that have flown back "home": what could be simpler? Yet in this very simplicity lies a feeling of the most intense life, almost of sanctification. There is not the slightest indication of his seeking a striking effect; only the transparency of the color, and the nobility of the color scale.

The greatest of landscape painters was Savrasov's pupil, I. Levitan (Plates 68, 69, 70). Great love and understanding of nature are needed to capture its essence, as Levitan does in his paintings. Every portion of his landscapes is full of life. There is no sense of stage scenery or background, as so often with landscapes in paintings. The magic of the resplendent farewell celebration that precedes the winter sleep is amazingly rendered in *The Golden Autumn. The Pool* makes one feel the mysterious depth, overflowing with life, of that calm, apparently commonplace water. The secret of Levitan's art lies in the fact that he has nothing commonplace. The "commonplace" is alive with cosmic life, revealed by the artist.

At the beginning of his artistic career, Levitan was a member of The Society of Itinerant Exhibitions. Later, he joined "The World of Art"—a group formed in 1890, which came to replace the Itinerants. Its moving spirit, in large measure was Diaghilev, who must be given the credit of making Russian art widely known in western Europe through his productions of the ballet, which were presented in all the large cities of Europe and America. The best artists of "The World of Art" group participated in those productions, and drew sketches for the stage sets and costumes.

FREE REALISM

This group promulgated what one of its founders, Alexander Benois (Plate 88), an excellent artist and a man of high European culture, calls "Free Realism." (We should rather have called it enlightened or cultured individualism). It was a cult of highly developed individuality. The painter was expected, first of all, to be original and free in the expression of his creative individuality, as well as perfect in his craftsmanship.

These qualities were possessed in the highest degree by M. Vrubel, whose work, on the threshold of the 20th century, represents one of the peaks in the achievement of Russian art. Ideologically, especially in his earlier years, he is closest to A. Ivanov, in spite of the entirely different manner in which the influence of Byzantium (of the icon painter, Theophanos, one of the progenitors of Russian painting) is combined with "the last word in technique" of impressionism. The luxuriant colors of Venice, where Vrubel spent several fruitful years, are also reflected in the gamut of his tones. Strong in Vrubel's art is also the Russian motif. His *Mikula Selianinovich* is a peasant hero, one of those that dwell unobserved in every Russian village, an embodiment of integral, native might. Russian nature is astonishingly embodied in Vrubel's *Pan* (Plate 79)—not an emigrant from the Greek Parnassus, but the very spirit of the Russian forest, alive with the breath of Russian soil and trees.

It is difficult to define in a few words the tendency of Vrubel's complex art. He possesses realism, in that his painting represents the knowledge of real, material forms of life. But his brush rendered also that which appeared to him beyond such life—something at times incredible in its scintillating fantasy, alternately tender (*Princess Dream; Czarevna Swan*) and awesome (*Demon; Ezekiel's Vision*) (Plate 80). Vrubel's images are symbolic—not, however, in the sense of a dry intellectual symbol, but in the way a mystic's emotions are symbolic.

The same is fully applicable to N. Roerich (Plates 81, 82), inwardly a much better balanced artist, but more one-sided as a painter. He started with an enthusiastic representation of Russian antiquity—a search for sources. He accepted as such sources religious art: first, before Russia's conversion to Christianity, the art of pagan worship; then, Christian art. But "the sign of Christ" led him, not to Byzantium, but the ancient lands of Tibet, China, and India, to which his art of the later period and of the present is exclusively dedicated.

There is a touch of mysticism in the art of N. Churlianis, the painter-musician (Plate 83). This artist surged, within the ensemble of "The World of Art" group, like a not very loud, but daring and peculiarly sonorous, chord. Millioti, though he somewhat resembles Churlianis by a sort of musical quality in his colors, was, however, more of a romantic than a mystic and symbolist.

In Russian art, the religious quest is almost invariably followed by a deeper penetration into Russian antiquity and life. This is brilliantly apparent in the art of V. Vasnetzov and M. Nesterov. Vasnetzov (Plates 73, 74, 75) loved Russian churches with their unique architecture. The faces of his saints are those of the Russian people, whose fairy-tales and legends were as dear to him as the lives of the saints. Nesterov (Plates 76, 77) transferred the popular saints into the environment of Russian landscape, of which he was a great master.

The line of popular art was followed by many other painters of "The World of Art"—Davidov, Maliutin, Helen Polenova, Marya Yakunchikova (Plate 106), and particularly I. Bilibin, who withdrew completely into old Russia. Bilibin (Plate 104) was the foremost expert of the Russian style, an outstanding specialist of popular art. His knowledge found practical application in connection with theatrical scenery and costumes (as, for instance, the remarkable staging of the opera, *Czar Saltan*), and illustrations of Russian fairy-tales. Those illustrations are highly imaginative and colorful, yet realistic and humorous.

The painter and architect, G. Lukomsky (Plate 105), knew well, and had the high artistic ability to depict, the original beauty of Russian architecture, ecclesiastical and secular. He has also made important contributions—documental and historical—to the literature of art.

The art of F. Maliavin (Plate 98), who all his life painted the Russian village woman, her broad-cheeked smile and the bright chintzes of her flowing garments, owes much to Impressionism. Impressionism had restored to painters the understanding of color, and cleansed it from the blackness that had afflicted the Itinerants, who paid little attention to "the trifles of beauty."

The foremost exponents of Impressionism in Russia were I. Tsionglinsky, P. Kontchalovsky, and I. Grabar (Plate 101). Russian art owes to Grabar many works on the history of art and monographs on individual painters. We find in Arkhipov (Plate 99), who has much in common with Maliavin in technique and subject, the harmonious blend of two apparently contradictory tendencies—the striving of the Itinerants for subject and episode, and that of the Impressionists towards the fleeting joy of ocular impressions. The same qualities mark the art of Braz, Pasternak (Plate 100), and Kustodiev.

Kustodiev (Plate 107) sought color in the life of the village, with its gay festivities and fairs; and in the life of the merchants, with their highly polished samovars, gold framed icons and rich garments. V. Borisov-Musatov (Plate 94) liked to depict the past of the Russian manor, which acquired under his brush and through the prism of time the poetry of subtlest nuances of color and psychology. The nacreous fluctuations of his colors show the influence of the French, in particular, of Puvis-de-Chavannes.

M. Dobujinsky (Plates 92, 93) was also fond of the Russian manor. He was a subtle painter, with a great mastery of line and a cultivation of color correspondencies. Gravitating as he did towards clarity of outline, a subtle simplicity of technique, and the black and white of book illustrations, Dobujinsky is a typical representative of the "Petersburgschool." This was a school of "graphics," as opposed to the Moscow school of "painters" who loved the irrepressible brightness of color, and a full, thick stroke of brush. The love of completion in line and tone showed itself also in Dobujinsky's sketches for the theater, as for example, those for *A Month in the Country* and *The Queen of Spades*, which are in themselves complete, independent paintings.

Among designers were S. Chekhonin, and G. Narbut, pupil of Bilibin; also, A. Ostroumova-Lebedeva, whose Petersburg engravings are full of charm.

Masters of portraits were Z. Serebriakova and S. Sorin (Plate 97).

Excellent colorists were K. Yuon, N. Sapunov (who regrettably died while still quite young), S. Sudeikin (Plate 108), P. Kuznetzov, M. Saryan (Plate 129), and B. Anisfeld. Kuznetzov and Saryan found inspiration in the colorfulness of the Orient; Sudeikin, in that of the provinces of central Russia, as did also Yuon. In the art of the latter, however, the influence of the French school is much stronger. Anisfeld's art contains a great deal of fantastic decorativeness—a quality that found application in his stage settings for the theater.

Much has been achieved in the realm of theatrical scenery by K. Korovin, L. Bakst, and A. Golovin, each of whom is remarkable in his own way. Golovin (Plate 103) was equally enthusiastic, especially in his younger years, about both Spain and Russian antiquity. This dual ardor is reflected in the gamut of his colors, wherein the love of deep contrasts—characteristic of the intensely emotional art of Spain—is coupled with the oriental, multicolored richness of Russian popular art. From this point of view it is interesting to compare two stage settings by Golovin—*Ruslan*, and *The Aragon Jota*. The latter, Golovin considered to be the best of his settings for the ballet. As the best of his stage settings for the opera, he deemed the *Orpheus*; for drama, *The Little Ejolf* by Ibsen. Golovin also was an excellent illustrator, as is manifest, for instance, in his illustrations for Hoffman's *Double-Ganger*.

What Spain meant to Golovin, France meant to Korovin (Plate 102). Perhaps his best paintings are those devoted to Paris, where he spent many years of his life, including his last years as an emigrant. Paris, which created the school of Impressionism—a city of nuances, of silvery fogs over the Seine, of sunny half-shadows—left an ineradicable imprint upon his art. But his life's work was dedicated to Russia, to the Russian theater. For many years, he served as official decorator for state theaters. Unfortunately, scenery does not last; it is to be regretted that Korovin did not rather apply his great talent to mural painting. The decorative panels he painted for the Paris World's Fair show how much he could have accomplished in that field. Korovin was also an excellent landscape painter.

The influence of the English artist, Aubrey Beardsley, is discernible in the masterful work of Bakst (Plate 84), in the skilful graphic quality of his theatrical sketches. At the same time, Bakst was a remarkable colorist. In the richness and newness of his color combinations he can perhaps be compared with Vrubel alone. That quality is fully revealed in his *Scheherezade*, one of the best stage settings of the Russian ballet.

Beardsley's influence was also felt by many other artists of "The World of Art": notably Dobujinsky (who, however, outgrew it in a very short time), E. Lanceray (Plates 90, 91), and Kalmakov. Subject to that influence, also, was Somov (Plate 89), who came, however, to create an original style, a world seen through the prism of the past, namely, of 18th century France. It is interesting to compare his work with that of the masters of that epoch, Boucher, Watteau, Fragonard. In many respects Somov is more delicate and subtle than they, but he naturally cannot possess their full vitality of the moment. His art belongs to the world of dreams. He resembles a highly intelligent and clever manager of a doll theater, whose fantasy is obeyed by magnificent dolls.

One of those—among the many ephemeral "individual styles" of that epoch—who preserved a wholesome stability was V. Serov (Plates 85, 86, 87). He, too, had passed through the phase of stylistic enthusiasms (for instance, the enthusiasm for the archaic in *The Rape of Europe*, which changed into a peculiar "cezanneism" in *The Portrait of Ida Rubinstein*). But he proved able to preserve a more objective view of the world, which permitted him to apprehend everything in a many-sided way, and excluded the danger of mannerism. His works are realistic in the best sense of the word, with "free" realism.

Somewhat apart in that group of Russian painters stands A. Yakovlev (Plate 95), one of the best draftsmen of the Russian school. He drew the way he breathed, with a natural ease. But behind that ease were concealed a firm schooling and great knowledge. That knowledge he was able to convey to others, possessing as he did the talents not only of an artist but of a teacher. He knew how to explain, how to show, how to arouse enthusiasm for work. Russian painters owe him a great deal; and not the Russians alone. He taught in academies and schools both in Europe and America. Another excellent teacher was V. Shukhayev (Plate 96), likewise a master of design and composition; also K. Petrov-Vodkin.

Petrov-Vodkin (Plates 109, 110, cover picture) is a versatile artist, complex and profound. He passed from the aesthetic individualism of "The World of Art" to a unique symbolism, based on a study of the primitives, with their austere truthfulness and simplicity. He filled that simplicity with a complex content. In its time the daring innovations of his painting, *Dream*, shown at an exhibition of "The World of Art," produced a minor revolution. Like Vrubel or Serov, Petrov-Vodkin remained independent of any school labels and, constantly changing and at the same time always remaining himself, betook his art and his knowledge into the contemporary, wholly different world of Soviet Russia.

And yet, that world is separated from the past by a complex period of breaking up—a tempestuous reconsideration of values.

FORMALISM

That reconsideration of values had started long before. As early as the beginning of the century, the south wind had brought from Italy, whence classicism once upon a time had also come, a new word: "futurism." In Italy, futurism was a rather clearly defined

 movement, directed against the stagnation that prevailed in the art of the land—the dusty silence of museums. To counterbalance that silence, the futurists made a lot of noise. Their founder and leader, the poet Marinetti, in one of his many manifestos described the content of the new movement as follows:

"We are young and our art is fiercely revolutionary."

There was no museum stillness in Russia at the time. Nevertheless the fiercely revolutionary ideas of the futurists met with a warm response in the hearts of young artists always eager for the "new," and also somewhat tired of the excessive aestheticism of some of the artists of "The World of Art." At first, under the name of "futurism," everyone came forward who pleased and in any way he pleased. The universally acknowledged leaders of futurism were the poet V. Mayakovsky—whose yellow blouse with black stripes—his formal attire on the stage—seemed in its time to be the banner of the art of the future—and D. Burliuk. The latter was recognized by a ring in his right ear. The futurists' slogans, however, especially in regard to art, were indefinite. "To enrich the world with new beauty, the beauty of speed" (an expression of Marinetti's) —was a statement which in practice did not suffice to create a new movement in the art of painting.

Before the end of World War I the new ideas were taken up by the group called "The Jack of Diamonds." It attempted to combine new ideas, both of domestic and foreign origin, under the slogan "pure form." But the various ideas were too contradictory, and the group fell apart. In its place appeared several small groups, such as "The Union of Leftists," "Four Arts," "The Blue Rose." The majority of painters who joined these groups belonged to schools of the so-called left. The moderates joined the Moscow "Society of Russian Artists," wherein the realistic tendency predominated.

The basic school of the left movement consisted of cubists—the heirs of the school of Cezanne. Their progenitors were: in France, Picasso; in Russia, Kandinsky. Later,

Kandinsky migrated to Western Europe, and his name is connected with European (German and French) schools. To the same school belonged Alexandra Exter (Plate 114), who produced many remarkable stage sets in the leftist style, and N. Altman (Plate 112) (one of his best-known works was the portrait of the poetess, Anna Akhmatova, painted in green-blue cold tones, which represented an excellent likeness in spite of its cubist treatment); also Lissitzky, Iohanson, Shternberg, Mitulin, and others.

Cubism was a sort of anatomical theater where, in search of "pure form," the fluent multiplicity of vital forms was divided, dissected and brought close to the three "basic" forms, the cube, the sphere and the cone, or their projections upon flat surfaces—square, circle and triangle. In their own way, the cubists knew how to draw, possessed in the highest degree the knowledge of the laws of composition, both in color and line, and in most cases were deeply devoted to art. But none of this could completely replace the work of the Academy, whose very dust they tried to wipe off their hands; and the lack of the simplest academic knowledge—of perspective, anatomy and ocular discipline— often remained a lifetime drag on the artist's work.

Narrowly connected with cubism, by the bonds of succession, was constructivism —an attempt to transfer the artist's field of action from the flat surface into space. The constructivists produced mosaics by mounting flat representations (pieces of paintings, photographs, newspaper clippings) together with three-dimensional objects, as well as complex schematic structures projecting the new world. Their leader was V. Tatlin (Plate 122). K. Malevitsh, together with Rodchenko, Klein, Sutin and others, founded the school of suprematists. "Standing on the borderline of transition from the physical plane to the astral" (in the expression of O. Beskin, in his article *Formalism in Painting*, published by Vsekhudozhnik, Moscow, 1933), the suprematists endeavored, consciously or unconsciously, to penetrate into the subconscious, enclose it with a line and color it. Close to them stood the expressionists, who stated openly: "Dematerialization is the aim of the world"—a statement, needless to say, neither new, nor lacking in interest. But in painting it led to a black square on a white background—a dead end.

In addition to those large groups, there were many small ones, variations of the former. For instance, "rayism," founded by Gontcharova (Plate 113) and Larionov, was a variation of cubism, as was also the later group of "Analytical Painting" (P. Filonov (Plate 124) and others). "The Subjectless" (Sutin, Klein (Plate 123)) were an outgrowth of suprematism. "Intuitivists" (Tishler (Plate 126), Labas, and others) and "Neo-Primitivists" (A. Drevin (Plate 125) and others) stood close to expressionism. All these groups came under the designation of "Formalists."

That term came into existence in the 1920's and was applied to all "fiercely revolutionary" leftist groups, starting with the futurists. Formalism means the exaltation of form at the expense of content. Ironically, the point of departure of the leftist movement was precisely their contempt for form. Painters abjured "the antiquated classical form" which seemed to them too material, in order to pursue what they called "cognition." They sought "the highest content"—the manifestation of the hidden rhythm of "absolute color," "the metaphysical subject," "the super-nature." They proudly declared: "The art of the past was only an embryo of ourselves." And all this finally reduced itself to form, to the symbolic black square on a white background. Form had avenged itself by passing their art to their descendants under the label of Formalism.

After the revolution of 1917, power and leadership in art were at first seized by the leftists. The Imperial Academy of Art was closed and replaced by the "Free College of Art." In practice this change consisted in ejecting the professors of the old school who had lived in the Academy and turning over the studios for the free use of pupils and leftists. Boasted the youths: "We have taken by storm the Bastille of the Academy." The Moscow School of Art was renamed *Vkhutemas*—a composite word which stood for "Higher Art Workshops."

But the leftists' honeymoon did not last long. Their art was individualistic, did not lend itself to social discipline and did not coincide with either the ideology or the aims of the revolutionary proletariat. It was an art of the few, incomprehensible and, seemingly, wholly useless even to the majority of the intelligentsia, to say nothing of the masses.

"THE REBUILDING" (THE EPOCH OF TRANSITION)

In 1921 Lenin in his manifesto condemned "the puerilities of the leftists." A regular campaign ("organized indignation") against the leftists began. The Formalists were a useless growth on "the artistic commonalty" of Soviet Russia and they were invited to "rebuild themselves." Those that either did not want or were unable to do so, left the country, to merge with the art of western Europe. Among these were Kandinsky, Chagal, Sutin. Those that remained proceeded honestly to rebuild themselves, refashion their ideology, and work in accordance with the place allotted to them in "the artistic commonalty." It was not a bad place. The state, which wanted to educate the masses and lure them to "the work of construction," understood what a mighty auxiliary force in that work is represented by art, what a powerful instrument of education and suggestion the artist can be. The immediate need was attractive publicity, and here it was that futurism with its fierce eloquence found political application. Mayakovsky and Lebedev created a new type of artistic poster, the success of which was very great. Such posters, on subjects of the latest news, were displayed in the windows of the Russian Telegraph Agency (ROST). They were produced by the simple and speedy means of stenciled cliché; hand-colored in them were combined picture and verse, both effectively planned and executed. The same type of poster was used with equally great success in World War II.

The constructivists, headed by Tatlin, devoted themselves to industrial and architectural design. The suprematist, Malevitsh, found an application for his talent for colors and knowledge of composition in designing majolicas and fabrics. Rodchenko began to produce book illustrations and stage sets for the movies. Easel painting, in those first post-revolutionary years, became almost extinct. Such painting requires individual concentration, calm, even solitude. All this was unattainable in the years of the advent of the masses, of grandiose common endeavor.

By contrast, the theater was overflowing with life. As a means for the education of the masses, the theater was indispensable. It is much easier to explain something to the public through the lips of an actor than in the pages of a book. Moreover, the theater had preserved a degree of realism even when the leftist enthusiasm in art was at its height, since it is directly connected with the human body, which lives and moves on its stage. In his book, *Encounters and Impressions*, quoted above, Golovin observes:

"It is not possible to alter the figures of human beings. While every style can be subject to any alteration, to any grotesquerie, there is nothing one can do with the human body. There is nothing left for the innovators but to agree to a compromise." And he complains that "occasionally one sees sketches for leftist stage settings in which costumes are entirely impossible of realization; as, for instance, the head placed somewhere to the side, in back of the shoulders, etc."

Posters, industrial art, theater—all this absorbed the boiling energy of the young during the first post-revolutionary years. The grandiose construction that started in the land united the artists under the slogan "Social Commission." In spite of the narrowing framework of that slogan and the obligatory requirement of a materialistic philosophy of life, there was a valid aspect to the situation. The "social commission" returned art—which had become lost in the realm of expressionistic guesses about the unknown and the soullessness of abstractions, of constructivist diagrams—to the source of vital sources, the soil. The social commission restored the lost discipline of the school. In order to depict convincingly the triumphs of the revolution (for instance, the work of a tiller of the soil, with the help of a new machine), one had first of all to know how to draw. One had to know anatomy, perspective, the whole academic code rejected and forgotten by the leftists who, seized with the ecstasy of destruction, despised the school.

It became necessary to study drawing, often starting with the very rudiments. Teachers were in demand.

Teachers were ready. Artists, such as Petrov-Vodkin, Brodsky (Plates 133, 134) and Lebedev (in Leningrad) and Favorsky, Gerassimov (Plate 137), Iohanson, Kuprianov (in Moscow) undertook to train the young. Later, they were joined by Bilibin and Shukhayev, who had returned from emigration. One of Favorsky's pupils is A. Deineka. Shmarinov and Boyim are pupils of Gerassimov; Pakhomov and Charushin, of Lebedev. A. Samokhvalov (Plates 140, 141, 142), one of the most original artists of Soviet Russia, is a pupil of Petrov-Vodkin.

In the middle of the 1920's there was formed the "Association of Artists of the Revolution" (AKHR), which took as its aim the coordination of the work of the artists with the general line of revolutionary and post-revolutionary work. A group came to be called a "brigade," which emphasized its place in the task of social construction. The brigades organized exhibitions showing the social-artistic attainments of the artists. AKHR was joined by many painters of the former Society of Moscow Artists, including Gerassimov, who at the present time is one of the leaders of Soviet art; also, Mashkevich, Ryndin, Maximov, Chernyshev, Shestakov.

In 1932 the Academy of Art was restored on new principles. An artist of great technical knowledge became its head, a former member of "The World of Art," Isaac Brodsky. Brodsky was one of the few academicians who had remained in Russia. The position he took can be defined by the words of Golovin: "A sense of proportion—this is the main thing in art. Where proportion is not observed, there is no art, or bad art." The fruitfulness of that formula in the realm of artistic training cannot be denied.

"SOCIAL REALISM"

The first attempts at the restoration of academic painting proved very weak. Viewed as paintings, the canvases represent the work of beginners, which, however, is but natural; they were in fact beginners. Best of all are the drawings from life, the clear-cut, "businesslike" paintings—representations of factories and farming, sketches and paintings of scientific expeditions (for instance, the majestic Arctic landscape by A. Merkulov: *The Power Station in the Arctic*).

Stalin has designated the trend of art in contemporary Russia as "social realism." "Social," communal, as contrasted with the "individual." Society, group—not an individual personality—this is what is now of concern.

Social realism is a successor to the realism of genre and subject, of the epoch of the Itinerants. In accordance with the times, the theme of social struggle was replaced with that of social construction. But the artist is almost completely controlled by the theme.

He simply has no time to think of anything else. He is accountable—his "line" is checked and "straightened out" (by means of a reprimand and a sermon) if it does not happen to coincide with the ideology and system of work of the State. The State Committee for the Affairs of Art, established and appointed by the Council of People's Commissars, sees to that. It organizes exhibitions, grants subsidies and stipends, manages the funds appropriated by the state for art. It also supervises schools, theaters, and clubs.

Artists are organized in trade unions, clubs, and cooperatives, based on the elective principle. The cooperative organization Vsekhudozhnik (All-Artist), which includes all artistic organizations and groups, serves as a mediator between the trade unions and the clients, chief among whom is the State. The so-called "creative alliances" are clubs in which are discussed matters of art, methods of work, and ideological questions. The State Committee for the Affairs of Art maintains a direct contact with those clubs.

Among the groups which joined the Vsekhudozhnik was the "Society of Easel Painters." The rebirth of easel painting began with the first signs that the country's political life was calming down. Some of the first post-revolutionary easel paintings were portraits of statesmen, as, for instance, of Lenin and Stalin, Voroshilov and others by Gerassimov. Later, paintings of composition, reflecting Soviet life, began to appear in constantly greater numbers. Landscapes also have gradually found their place in art. Among the artists were the masters of landscape, M. Nesterov and A. Rylov. Their influence, as well as the beneficial influence of Levitan, left its mark on young painters, such as A. Rzheznikov, L. Zevin, A. Morozov. G. Nissky chose as his specialty the "industrial landscape." In his paintings nature is touched by the human hand—billows of smoke from factory chimneys vie with the clouds in the sky, and against the background of forests and fields rise silhouettes of factories, engines, machines.

Petrov-Vodkin, Brodsky, Lebedev, Nesterov (who exchanged his mystical search for a psychological one and produced a series of excellent, deeply meaningful, and masterly portraits), Kontchalovsky (who developed in the direction of realism, as did also Iohanson) always were and remain easelers. They were joined by Gerassimov, P. Williams (Plate 121), Deineka, Kukryniksi (Plate 143) (the latter is a collective name used as a signature by Kuprianov, Krylov and N. Sokolov); Antonov, Boyim, Samokhvalov, Riazhsky, Korin (Plate 135).

By the 1930's, artistic construction was in full bloom. Over the country's whole expanse academies began to appear, for instance, the national academies of the Ukraine, Uzbekistan, Turkestan, Georgia.

Young people from the Siberian tundra and the islands of the Arctic Ocean came to the Leningrad Institute of Northern Peoples to study arts and sciences. Later, upon returning home, they began to teach others. At the exhibition of 1939, arranged by the Institute, there was displayed the painting of the Nanaets (Plates 149, 150)—inhabitants of the far North. The landscapes and scenes from life depict an existence in the midst of stern, northern nature—rocks, sparse trees, snow, deer, human beings clad in animal hides. For the most part, the composition of those pictures is good, in sense of balance, rhythm, and the purity of a primitive. In the same year, Armenia, one of the component republics of the Soviet Union, celebrated the millennium of the Armenian national epic, the poem *David Sosunsky*. On that occasion there was published an anniversary edition of the poem with illustrations by the Armenian artist, Ashot Mamadzhanyan (Plates 151, 152). These drawings speak of the ancient Byzantine-Persian culture of Armenia, of elaborate architecture, magnificent garments. What a contrast with the art of the Nanaets, and how significant that both are parts of a single whole! How versatile, colorful, and rich can be the art of a country that unites within itself so many different traditions and schools!

At the same time the icon workshops of Palekh and Mstery have also opened their doors to secular art. The production of icons, however, had long since been reduced to a minimum and replaced by the development of the miniature. The lacquered boxes decorated by the Palekh artists were valued highly, not only at home but also abroad. In 1924 they were shown at an exhibition in Venice; two years later, at the International Exhibition in Paris. Their highly original art was deservedly appreciated. Together with praise, they were showered with orders. In 1939, an exhibition of their works was arranged in Moscow. One can judge by these exhibits the wide evolution of their art.

The tradition of icon painting still preserves its power in these miniatures. The composition is well-balanced, dynamic, thoroughly planned—each line is necessary in the common rhythm; each nuance, in the common gamut of colors. As great as in the past is the skill of applying the paint, bright and clear, radiant as on an icon. Some of the miniatures, such as *The Death of Susanin* (Plate 154) by Vatagin, or *The Fire Bird* (Plate 153) by Kotukhin, deserve a place of honor in a museum. In addition to the miniatures, there are already easel paintings signed by "Paleshane," like *Red Partisans* (Plate 155) by Golikov.

Some of the masters chose subjects of "social construction," such as *Celebrating the Harvest at a Collective Farm* (Plate 156) by Bakhirev. It is interesting to trace in this work the centuries-old, but still vital connection between the present and the past. The representation of houses on a village street reveals inheritance from Byzantine chapels; in the sky, above a stylized medieval tree, float clouds as on the icons. At the same time, one feels a realistic approach, an attentive attitude towards nature, the features of the human face, the characteristic details of life. The very well composed still-life with a samovar on the table and vegetables and fruits in the foreground, is quite realistic.

The Paleshane apply their art also to theatrical scenery, costumes, and book illustrations. In 1938, the state publishing house, Artistic Literature, issued a picture book, *Folk Tales of Old*. The refined drawings in this book represent the last word in the technique of illustration. And here an unexpected parallel must be drawn: those book illustrations by the folk artists of Palekh are very close to the art of "The World of Art" members—the refined illustrations by Bilibin, Dobujinsky, Somov, Bakst. "The World of Art?" Yes, a world of art grown and reared in the midst of the people themselves—a creative world which has fought its way through to freedom of individual creation.

Timidly at first, then louder and louder, sound the voices in defense of individuality. The theme of the value of individuality is gradually beginning to outweigh in criticism the ideological sermons and instructions. V. Kostin writes in his book, *Young Artists and the Problems of Soviet Art* (State Publishing House, Art, Moscow-Leningrad):

"An artist is born in pains, contradictions, struggle—in enormous, intense labor. His individuality is formed, like the works of a sculptor, from the inside, growing gradually, until a clear distinct image appears."

Further, analyzing the process of artistic creation, he writes of "the individual solution of all separate problems of a work's artistic form."

And toward the end of the 1930's a new era in the blossoming of the artistic life of the U.S.S.R. became apparent. Many cultural institutions are now at work in the land, and new ones keep arising. The State Publishing House, Art, publishes a series of popular books on art, both Russian and foreign. These books, accessible to the mass of the people in both price and manner of presentation, are produced with taste. It is characteristic that this publishing house continued to function in war-time. The small book by Alpatiev on Andrew Rublev (surely a non-military theme!) is dated with the war year 1943.

Before the war, the attendance at galleries and exhibitions grew extraordinarily. The figures of attendance at the Tretyakov Gallery (Plate 164) in Moscow are revealing: in 1913—150,000 visitors; in 1928—265,000; and during the pre-war years—900,000.

Exhibitions of Russian art are organized both in Russia itself and abroad. Artists receive subsidies for foreign travel. Many Soviet artists have visited Europe, especially Paris; and America. A. Deineka was awarded first prize at the international exhibition in Pittsburgh (United States) for his painting, *Girl on a Balcony*.

Deineka (Plate 138) is one of the most notable and characteristic representatives of contemporary Soviet art. He was born in 1893, in the family of a Kursk railroad official, and received his first education in art at the Kharkov Art School. There he came somewhat under the influence of leftists, but just enough to learn from them "the courage of daring," as well as the art of composition and skill in handling the instruments and materials of production. After the Revolution, which he greeted with an outburst of enthusiasm (as attested by his article in a 1919 issue of the magazine *Our Day*), he worked in Moscow in *Vkutemas* (Higher Art Technical Workshops)—the former Moscow School of Art—under the artist Favorsky. Later, he went over to the Society of Easelers and still later, to the society "October." During his trip abroad he became enthusiastic about the art of France and Italy, and especially about construction in America. His art is versatile and sincere. Occasionally, it is too monolithic and poster-like (as in his pictures of sports and of war, such as *Artillery Attacking*), but he possesses the means of emancipating himself from those characteristics. Most other Soviet painters are following the same road as Deineka. Samokhvalov, Kukryniksi, Sokolov-Skala, Boyim, Antonov (Plate 139), Pimenov, Riazhsky, Korin, Merkulov, Shmarinov, Dekhterev, Rodionov—all artists who differ in the degree of talent and the nuances of artistic education—are united by the ideology of "social realism."

The catastrophe of the Second World War, which burst over the land with inconceivable cruelty and devastation, did not stop the artists' work. Being a part of the country's social order, of the habitual and necessary routine of life and education, art continued its service. In the front-line, as in the rear, artists went on with their work. Documentary in character, frighteningly eloquent, are the front-line sketches of D. Shmarinov (collected in his album *We Will Not Forget*) (Plates 161, 162), and N. Zhukov (Plate 159), and the engravings of B. Blank (Plate 160). Deineka paints pictures on military subjects, which, however, are little characteristic of him. Interesting in its composition is the collective work of Yakovlev, Shukhmin and Sokolov-Skala: *Battle at Moscow* (Plate 158).

At the beginning of the war, when nearly all Russia became the immediate rear of the fighting line, the art treasures were taken from museums to Siberia. Part of the building of the Tretyakov Gallery was demolished in the bombardment of Moscow. But no sooner did the enemy retreat from the city's walls than the work of reconstruction began, and even in 1943 exhibitions were opened in the renovated halls. In another year, the Gallery was completely rebuilt, and the paintings, safely returned from Siberia, put back in place. The reopening of the Gallery was celebrated with solemn festival.

The wave of passionate patriotism that swept the land gave a new impetus to Soviet art. The yoke of the obligatory "social commission" was replaced by a free elan, which restored to the artist his freedom of initiative. The "social commission" had robbed him of that quality—had robbed him of the possibility of searching for the new in the unknown, for he had been given a ready-made ideology. Everything had to be known to him, to be clear without any doubt.

But the artist is, first of all, an explorer in the field of the unknown, in the fruitful depths of consciousness where artistic creation has its roots; and for the sake of art, the true inner freedom, the liberty of choice, is essential.

The war swept something away. To some extent, the change of subject produced its effect. Or perhaps, the time had already come; for the new, more artistic approach had been ripening before the war. There are many talented artists in the U.S.S.R. The state welcomes them, encourages the art school, encourages talent. And steadily clearer become the outlines of a new school to which the future belongs. That school is built on a sound foundation. An artist is required to possess a knowledge of his craft and a cultural background, as well as to participate in the common endeavor. All this leads to a search for some kind of objectivity, which is a positive factor. It contains also a great deal of idealism which, for the most part, is characteristic of the productions of Russian art of all periods and trends.

V. Kostin speaks of "great heights" which the artist must strive to attain: "We are the true heirs to everything best bequeathed by human culture. We want our art, like the art of the classics, to evoke excitement and love, so that in it people will find an immense vitality of theme, a true mastery of form, force and beauty. Our painting must be rich, sonorous, varied. It must speak of the fate of human beings, their struggle, their remarkable aims. It must assist the birth of great human consciousness, great ideas and strong emotions." There is every indication that Soviet art is effectively moving toward these goals.

BIBLIOGRAPHY

BENOIS, A.: The Russian School of Painting. St. Petersburg, 1904.

——: The Russian School of Painting. With introduction by Christian Brinton. A. Knopf, New York, 1916.

——: Museum Alexander III (now Russian State Museum at Leningrad). Knebel, Moscow, 1906.

RUNES, D., and SCHRICKEL, H.: Encyclopedia of the Arts. Philosophical Library, 1946.

GRABAR, I.: History of Russian Art. Edition Knebel, Moscow, 1909–1912.

MURATOV, P.: Les Icones Russes. Edition J. Schiffrin, Paris, 1927.

——: L'Ancienne Peinture Russe. Edition A. Stock, Rome-Prague, 1925.

USPENSKY, A.: Russian Painting of 15th–18th Centuries. Moscow, 1906.

ROVINSKY, D.: Russian Popular Pictures. (5 volumes.)

KONDAKOV, N.: The Russian Icon. (Translated by H. Minns.) Clarendon Press, Oxford, 1927.

ANISSIMOV, A.: Theophane le Grec (La peinture russe de XIV siècle). Gazette des Beaux Arts, Paris. 1930.

AVINOFF, A.: The Russian Icon: Its History and Characteristics. Carnegie Institute, Pittsburgh, 1944.

VIKHREV, Y.: Palekh Artists. State Publishing House for Fiction and Poetry, Moscow, 1938.

RÉAU, LOUIS: L'Art Russe de Pierre le Grand à Nos Jours (Ouvrage publié sous le patronage de l'Institut d'Etudes Slaves à Paris). H. Laurens, éditeur. Paris, 1922.

SAVINOV, A.: Russian State Museums, "Iskusstvo," Leningrad, 1939.

Album published by K. Fisher, Moscow, 1897, for 25-year jubilee of "Wanderers."

BRINTON, CHRISTIAN: The Ilya Repin Exhibition and Catalogue of Painting. Kingore Galleries, New York, 1921.

GOLOVIN, A.: Encounters and Impressions. "Iskusstvo," Moscow-Leningrad, 1940.

TAGER, E., RIKHENSTEIN, M., and ZOTOV, N., under redaction of N. Sokolova: Russian Art. "Iskusstvo," Moscow-Leningrad, 1938.

SALMON, ANDRÉ: Art Russe Moderne. Edition Laville, Paris, 1928.

MARTINO: Le Futurisme. Paris, 1922.

KANDINSKY, V.: The Art of Spiritual Harmony. (Translated by Sadler.) Boston, 1914.

BESKIN, O.: Formalism in Painting. Moscow, 1933.

GALUSHKINA, A., and PETROV-VODKIN, K.: Ogiz. State Publishing House for Pictorial Arts, Moscow, 1936.

CHEN, JACK: Soviet Art and Artists. Chiswick Press, London, 1944.

KOSTIN, V.: The Young Artists and the Problems of Soviet Art. "Iskusstvo," Moscow-Leningrad, 1940.

ZAMOSHKIN, A., and GERASSIMOV, A., "Iskusstvo," Moscow-Leningrad, 1936.

ALPATOV, M., and RUBLEV, A., "Iskusstvo," Moscow-Leningrad, 1943.

LEBEDEV, A., and REPIN, I., "Iskusstvo," Moscow-Leningrad, 1944.

NEDOSHIVIN, T., and FEDOTOV, P., "Iskusstvo," Moscow-Leningrad, 1945.

INDEX OF ILLUSTRATIONS

64. I. Repin: Tolstoy on the Ploughfield.
65. I. Repin: Ivan the Terrible and His Son Ivan (detail).
66. V. Surikov: The Exile of Boyarinia Morozova.
67. V. Surikov: Menshikov in Exile.
68. I. Levitan: Above the Eternal Rest.
69. I. Levitan: Grass-grown Pond.
70. I. Levitan: Deep Waters.
71. A. Kuindzhi: Birch Grove.
72. I. Ostroukhov: Windy Day.
73. V. Vasnetzov: Alyonushka.
74. V. Vasnetzov: Three Russian Knights—Bogatyri.
75. V. Vasnetzov: The Last Judgment.
76. M. Nesterov: Vision of St. Bartholomew.
77. M. Nesterov: Portrait of Sculptress Vera Mukhina.
78. A. Vasnetzov: Moscow in 17th Century.
79. M. Vrubel: Pan.
80. M. Vrubel: Defeated Demon.
81. N. Roerich: Higher Than the Mountains.
82. N. Roerich: Book Out of Heaven.
83. N. Churlianis: The Pyramids.
84. L. Bakst: Terror Antiquus.
85. V. Serov: Girl in Sunlight.
86. V. Serov: October.
87. V. Serov: Portrait of Composer Rymsky-Korsakov.
88. A. Benois: Versailles.
89. K. Somov: Promenade of Marquise.
90. E. Lanceray: Promenade of Empress Elisabeth I.
91. E. Lanceray: St. Petersburg at the Time of Peter the Great.
92. M. Dobujinsky: Man with Eyeglasses.
93. M. Dobujinsky: Silence. (From the series, "Visions of the City.")
94. V. Borisov-Musatov: At the Pond.
95. A. Yakovlev: Gaden Elephant Hunter.
96. V. Shukhayev: Portrait of Mrs. L.
97. S. Sorin: Russian Peasant.
98. F. Maliavin: Portrait.
99. A. Arkhipov: A Peasant Woman.
100. L. Pasternak: Circle of Moscow Painters.
101. I. Grabar: Azure Sky in February.
102. K. Korovin: Paris at Night.
103. A. Golovin: Spanish Girl on the Balcony.
104. I. Bilibin: Golden Rooster. Illustration to a fairy tale.

105. G. Lukomsky: Ancient Cathedral.
106. Mary Yakunchikova: Church Bells.
107. B. Kustodiev: Merchant's Wife Drinking Tea.
108. S. Sudeikin: Shrove-Tide.
109. K. Petrov-Vodkin: Girl at the Window.
110. K. Petrov-Vodkin: Self-portrait.
111. B. Grigoriev: Portrait.
112. N. Altman: Woman's Head.
113. Nathalie Gontcharova: Spanish Women.
114. Alexandra Exter: Bridge.
115. G. Annenkov: Portrait of A. Tikhonov.
116. G. Annenkov: Self-portrait.
117. I. Puni: Still Life.
118. M. Chagal: Sketch.
119. Mane Katz: King of Carnival.
120. N. Glushchenko: Landscape.
121. P. Williams: Portrait of Mayerhold.
122. V. Tatlin: Monument to the Third International.
123. I. Klein: Suprematism.
124. P. Filonov: Living Head.
125. A. Drevin: Deer.
126. A. Tishler: Woman and Airplane.
127. A. Shevtshenko: Fisherman's Children.
128. K. Istomin: Morning.
129. M. Saryan: My Family.
130. P. Kontchalovsky: Katenka.
131. A. Rylov: Summer Day.
132. K. Bogayevsky: Landscape.
133. I. Brodsky: Winter Landscape.
134. I. Brodsky: Lenin in Smolny.
135. P. Korin: Portrait of Maxim Gorky.
136. V. Yakovlev: Goldseekers Writing a Letter to the Creator of the Great Constitution.
137. A. Gerassimov: In the Bath-house.
138. A. Deineka: Shower Baths.
139. F. Antonov: Love
140. A. Samokhvalov: Russian Girl.
141. A. Samokhvalov: Illustration to "History of the City" by Saltykov-Shchedrin.
142. A. Samokhvalov: "Khodia."
143. Kukryniksi: Bandit Makhno.
144. M. Kurilko working on his murals for the Siberian Pavillon of the All-Union Agricultural Fair in Moscow.
145. M. Kurilko: The Frog Princess. Illustration to a fairy tale. Watercolor.
146. Ishakevitsh: Kobzar (watercolor).

LIST OF ILLUSTRATIONS IN TEXT

LIST OF ARTISTS

Aivazovsky, I., 1817–1900
Akimov, I., 1754–1814
Altman, N., born 1889
Alexeiev, F., 1753–1804
Annenkov, G., born 1889
Antropov, A., 1716–1795
Antonov, A., contemporary
Anisfeld, B., born 1883
Argunov, I., 1727–1797
Arkhipov, A., 1862–1930
Bakst, L., 1878–1925
Bakhirev (Palekh artist), contemporary
Benois, A., born 1870
Blank, B., contemporary
Bogayevsky, K., born 1872
Borisov-Musatov, V., 1870–1905
Borovikovsky, V., 1757–1825
Bogdanov-Belsky, N., born 1868
Boyim, contemporary
Bryullov, K., 1799–1852
Brodsky, I., 1844–1938
Bruni, F., 1799–1875
Braz, born 1872
Burliuk, D., contemporary
Chagal, M., born 1887
Charushin, contemporary
Chekhonin, S., born 1878
Churlianis, N., 1875–1913
Deineka, A., born 1899
Dionysius (icon painter, end of 15th and beginning of 16th century)
Dobujinsky, M., born 1875
Drevin, A., born 1889
Exter, Alexandra, born 1884
Favorsky, V., born 1886
Fedotov, P., 1816–1852
Filonov, P., born 1883
Firsov, I., middle of 18th century
Flavitzky, K., 1830–1866
Gay, N., 1831–1894
Gagarin, Prince G., 1810–1895
Galaktionov, S., 1778–1854
Gaush, A., born 1873

Gaifedzhan, contemporary
Gerassimov, A., born 1884
Glushchenko, N., contemporary
Golikov, I. (Palekh artist), contemporary
Gontcharova, Nathalie, born 1883
Golovin, A., 1863–1930
Grabar, I., born 1871
Grigoriev, B., 1886–1938
Iohanson, contemporary
Ishakevitch, contemporary
Istomin, K., born 1887
Ivanov, A., 1806–1858
Kandinsky, V., born 1866
Katz, M., contemporary
Kalmakov, A., contemporary
Kazanetz, I., icon painter, second part of 17th century
Klein, I., contemporary
Kotukhin, A. (Palekh artist), contemporary
Kiprensky, O., 1783–1836
Kontchalovsky, P., born 1876
Korin, P., born 1892
Korovin, K., 1861–
Kondratiev, G., Palekh artist, second part of 17th century
Korovin, S., 1858–1908
Kramskoy, I., 1837–1887
Krylov, P., born 1902
Kustodiev, B., 1878–1927
Kurilko, M., contemporary
Kuindzhi, A., 1842–1910
Kuprianov, born 1903
Kuznetzov, P., born 1878
Lanceray, E., born 1875
Labas, contemporary
Levitan, I., 1861–1900
Levitzky, D., 1735–1822
Lebedev, M., 1812–1837
Lissitzky, contemporary
Lukomsky, G., born 1884
Losenko, A., 1737–1773
Marvina, Tatiana, contemporary
Mamadzhanyan, A., contemporary

Maliavin, F., born 1869

Makovsky, V., 1846–1920

Makovsky, K., 1839–1915

Maliutin, S., 1859–1937

Malevitsh, K., contemporary

Mashkov, I., born 1884

Maximov, contemporary

Merkulov, A., born 1904

Millioti, D., contemporary

Moscvitin, E., icon painter, Tzar Painters School, beginning of 17th century

Moller, F. von, 1812–1875

Mukhina, Vera (sculptress), born 1889

Narbut, G., 1886–1920

Neshensky, V., contemporary

Nesterov, M., 1862–1942

Nissky, G., born 1903

Ostroukhov, I., 1858–1929

Ostroumova-Lebedeva, A., born 1871

Pasternak, L., born 1862

Pakhomov, A., born 1900

Perov, V., 1833–1882

Petrov-Vodkin, K., 1878–1939

Polenov, V., 1844–1928

Polenova, Helen, 1850–1898

Poznansky, V., icon painter, end of 17th century

Pryanishnikov, I., 1840–1894

Puni, I., contemporary

Repin, I., 1844–1930

Riazhsky, G., born 1895

Roerich, N., born 1874

Rokotov, F., 1735–1808

Rodchenko, contemporary

Rodionov, M., born 1885

Rodionova, E., born 1912

Rublev, A., icon painter, end of 14th century and first half of 15th century.

Samokhvalov, A., born 1894

Savrasov, A., 1830–1897

Saryan, M., born 1881

Sapunov, N., 1880–1912

Savin, N., icon painter, Tzar Painters School, beginning of 17th century

Serov, V., 1865–1911

Semiradsky, G., 1843–1902

Serebriakova, Z., contemporary

Shibanov, M., second part of 18th century

Shevtchenko, T., national Ukrainian poet, first half of 19th century

Shevtchenko, A., born 1886

Shishkin, I., 1831–1898

Shmarinov, D., born 1907

Shukhayev, V., contemporary

Shukhmin, P., born 1894

Shebuyev, V., 1777–1855

Shchedrin, S., 1791–1830

Shternberg, contemporary

Shchirin, P., icon painter, Tzar Painters School, beginning of 17th century

Somov, K., 1869–1939

Sorin, S., born 1880

Sokolov-Skala, N., born 1899

Stelletzki, contemporary

Surikov, V., 1848–1916

Sutin, C., contemporary

Tatlin, V., born 1885

Terentyeva, M. (Nanaetz artist), contemporary

Theophanos, Greek icon painter, end of 14th century

Tishler, A., contemporary

Tolstoy, Prince F., 1783–1879

Tropinin, V., 1776–1857

Tsionglinsky, I., born 1858

Ugryumov, G., 1764–1823

Ushakov, S., icon painter, "Friaz" School, 1626–1686

Uza, V. (Nanaetz artist), contemporary

Vatagin (Palekh artist), contemporary

Vasnetzov, V., 1848–1926

Vasnetzov, A., 1856–1932

Venetzianov, A., 1780–1847

Vereshchiagin, V., 1842–1905

Vrubel, M., 1858–1910

Williams, P., born 1902

Yakovlev, A., 1887–1938

Yakunchikova, Mary, 1870–1903

Yaroshenko, N., 1846–1898

Yakoby, V., 1834–1902

Yuon, K., born 1875

Zarianko, 1818–1870

Zevin, contemporary

Zhukov, N., contemporary

1. Archangel Mikhail. Early XIV Century Icon.

27704

2. Trinity. Early XIV Century Icon.

3. A. Rublev. — Trinity. XV Century.

4. Painter Unknown. — Part Of The Mural (Fresco) Of The Blagoveshchensky Cathedral In Moscow. — These Murals Were Discovered During The Restoration In 1882. Later, They Were Painted Over, But Photographs Were Taken And Are In The Archives Of Court Department In Moscow.

5. Painter Unknown. — Philosopher. Part Of The Mural (Fresco) Of The
Blagoveshchensky Cathedral In Moscow.

6.   St. Demetrius. — Stroganov School Icon. — Late XVI Century.

7. N. Savin. — St. John The Baptist In The Desert. Early XVII Century.

8. Lubok. — Russian Folk Picture. XVIII Century. Temptation Of St. Anthony.

9. Lubok. — Russian Folk Picture. 1848. Illustration To A Folk Song.

10. A. Antropov. — Portrait Of A Man.

11.　G. Ugryumov. — Portrait Of The Merchant Vodovozov.

12. I. Akimov. — Saturn And Amour.

13.   F. Rokotov. — Portrait Of Empress Katherine II.

14. D. Levitzky. — Portrait Of Prince Golitzin.

15.   V. Borovikovsky. — Portrait Of Madame Lopukhina.

16. F. Alexeiev. — Neva Quai.

17. M. Shibanov. — Betrothal.

18.   F. Von-Moller. — Portrait of N. Gogol.

19. Prince G. Gagarin. — Georgian Woman.

20.   O. Kiprensky. — Portrait Of A Lady.

21. V. Tropinin. — Lace-Maker.

22.   V. Tropinin. — Portrait Of K. Bryullov.

23.   K. Bryullov. — Self-Portrait.

24.   K. Bryullov. — The Last Day Of Pompeii.

25. K. Bryullov. — Turkish Woman.

26. F. Bruni. — Madonna With Child.

27.   F. Bruni. — Bacchante.

28. K. Flavitzky. — Princess Tarakanova.

29.   A. Ivanov. — The Appearance Of Christ Before The People.

30.   A. Ivanov. — Head Of St. John The Baptist.   (Sketch).

31. A. Ivanov. — Annunciation. (Sketch).

32.   N. Gay. — Crucifixion.

33. N. Gay. — Golgotha.

THE LIBRARY
COLBY JUNIOR COLLEGE
NEW LONDON, N. H.

34. N. Gay. — Peter I And His Son Alexis.

35. I. Kramskoy. — Christ In The Desert.

36. I. Kramskoy. — Unknown.

37.   I. Kramskoy. — Portrait Of Leo Tolstoy.

38. V. Polenov. — Christ And The Sinner.

39. V. Polenov. — Moscow Back-Yard.

40. G. Semiradsky. — Frina At Eleusian Celebrations.

41. A. Venetzianov. — Barn.

42.   A. Venetzianov. — Peasant Lassie.

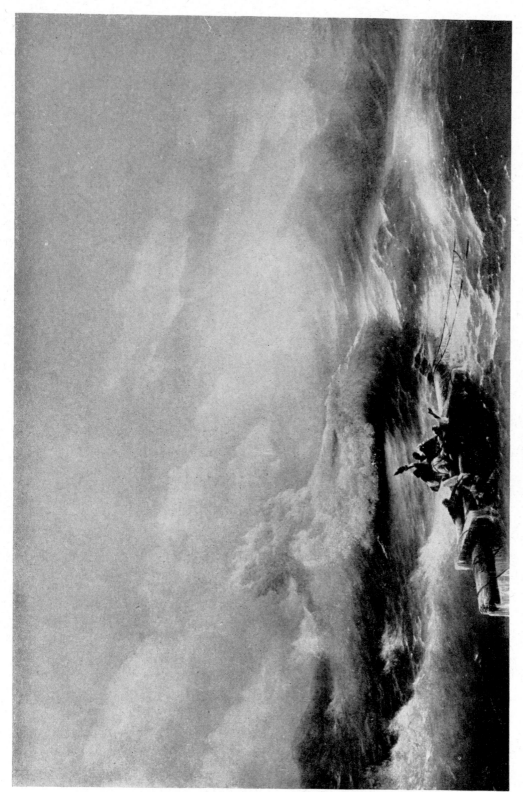

43.　I. Aivazovsky. — The Tidal Wave.

44. P. Fedotov. — Little Widow.

45. P. Fedotov. — The Major Comes To Woo.

46. V. Perov. — Arrival Of The Governess.

47. V. Perov. — The Hunters' Stories.

48.   V. Perov. — Portrait Of Dostoievsky.

49. I. Pryanishnikov. — What A Joke!

50. T. Shevtshenko. — The Landlord Exchanging People For Dogs.

51. K. Makovsky. — Children In Flight From The Thunderstorm.

52. K. Makovsky. — Alexeich.

53. N. Yaroshenko. — Stoker.

54. N. Yaroshenko. — Prisoner.

55. V. Vereshchagin. — Sudden Attack.

56.   V. Vereshchagin. — Apotheos Of The War.

57.   A. Savrasov. — The Rooks Have Come.

58. I. Shishkin. — Morning In The Pine Wood.

59. I. Shishkin. — Spider's Web In The Forest.

60. V. Makovsky. — Rendez-vous.

61. I. Repin. — Self Portrait.

62. I. Repin. — Cossacks Of Zaporozhye. — "Zaporozhtsy".

63. I. Repin. — Church Procession.

64. I. Repin. — Leo Tolstoy On The Ploughfield.

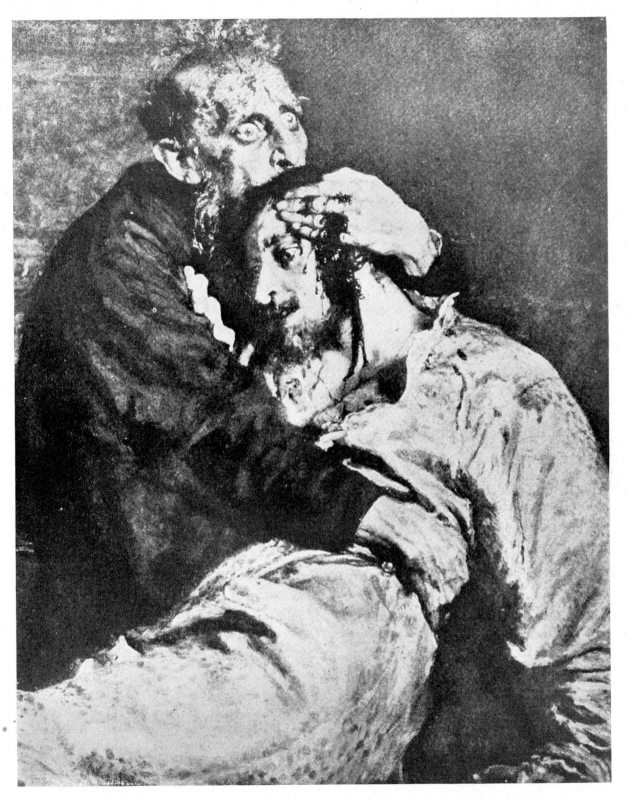

65. I. Repin. — Ivan The Terrible And His Son Ivan. (Detail).

66.   V. Surikov. — The Exile Of Boyarinia Morozova.

67. V. Surikov. — Menshikov In Exile.

68. I. Levitan. — Above The Eternal Rest.

69. I. Levitan. — A Grass-Grown Pond.

70. I. Levitan. — Deep Waters.

71. A. Kuindzhi. — Birch Grove.

72. I. Ostroukhov. — Windy Day.

73. V. Vasnetzov. — Alyonoushka.

74. V. Vasnetzov. — Three Russian Knights. — "Bogatyri".

75.   V. Vasnetzov. — The Last Judgment.

76. M. Nesterov. — Vision Of St. Bartholomew.

77. M. Nesterov. — Portrait Of The Sculptress V. Mukhina.

78. A. Vasnetzov. — Moscow In XVII Century.

79. M. Vrubel. — Pan.

80.　M. Vrubel. — Defeated Demon.

81. N. Roerich. — Higher Than The Mountains.

82. N. Roerich. — Book Out Of Heaven.

83. - N. Churlianis. — Pyramids.

84. L. Bakst. — Terror Antiquus.

85. V. Serov. — Girl In Sunlight.

86.   V. Serov. — October.

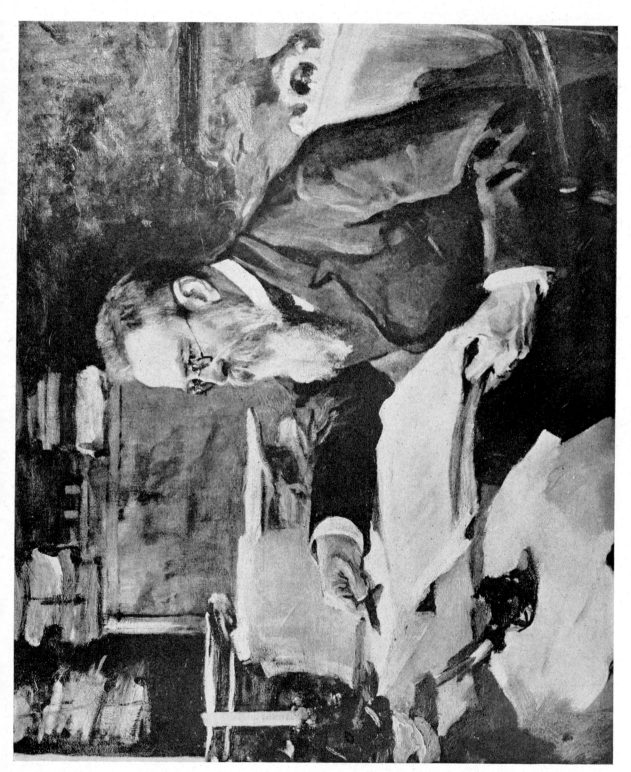

87. V. Serov. — Portrait Of Composer Rymsky-Korsakov.

88. A. Benois. — Versailles.

89.   K. Somov. — Promenade Of Marquise.

90.   E. Lanceray. — Promenade Of Empress Elisabeth I.

91.   E. Lanceray. — St. Petersburg At The Time Of Peter The Great.

92. M. Dobujinski. — Man With The Eye Glasses.

93. M. Dobujinsky. — Silence. (Series "Visions Of The City").

94. V. Borisov-Musatov. — At The Pond.

95. A. Yakovlev. — Gaden Elephant Hunter.

96.   V. Shukhayev. — Portrait Of Mrs. L.

99.   A. Arkhipov. — A Peasant Woman.

100. L. Pasternak. — Circle Of Moscow Painters.

101. I. Grabar. — Azure Sky In February.

102. K. Korovin. — Paris At Night.

103.   A. Golovin. — Spanish Girl On The Balcony.

104. I. Bilibin. — Golden Rooster. Illustration To A Fairy-Tale.

105. G. Lukomsky. — Ancient Cathedral.

106. Mary Yakunchikova. — Church Bells.

107. B. Kustodiev. — Merchant's Wife Drinking Tea.

108. S. Sudeikin. — Shrove-Tide.

109.   K. Pertov-Vodkin. — Girl At The Window.

110. K. Petrov-Vodkin. — Self-Portrait.

111. B. Grigoriev. — Portrait.

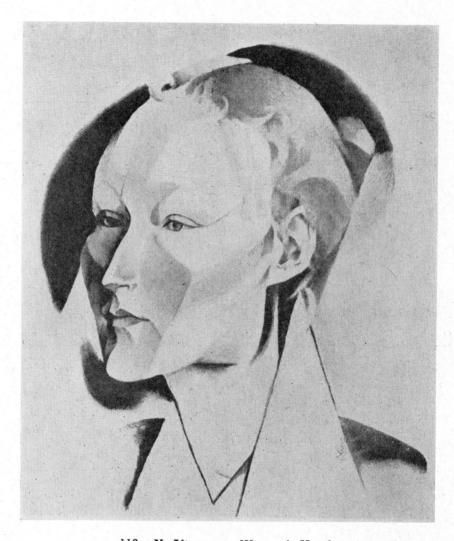

112. N. Altman. — Woman's Head.

113.   Nathalie Gontcharova. — Spanish Women.

114. A. Exter. — Bridge.

115. G. Annenkov. — Portrait Of A. Tikhonov.

116. G. Annenkov. — Self-Portrait.

117. I. Puni. — Still Life.

118. M. Chagal. — Sketch.

119.   Mane Katz. — King Of Carnival.

120. N. Glushchenko. — Landscape.

121. P. Williams. — Portrait Of Mayerhold.

122.   V. Tatlin. — Monument To The Third International.

123.   I. Klein. — Suprematism.

124. P. Filonov. — Living Head.

125. A. Drevin. — Deer.

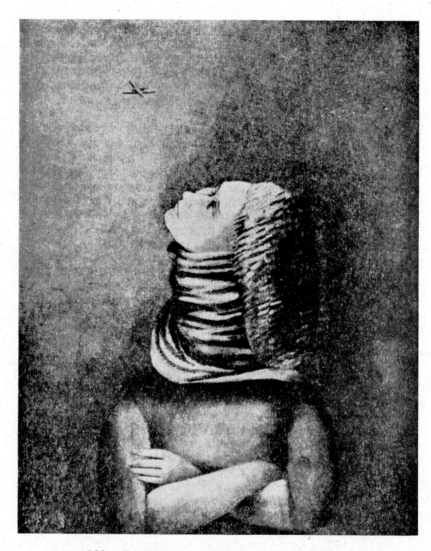

126.   A. Tishler. — Woman And Airplane.

127. A. Shevtshenko. — Fisherman's Children.

128.   K. Istomin. — Morning.

129. M. Saryan. — My Family.

130. P. Kontchalovsky. — Katenka.

131. A. Rylov. — Summer Day.

132. K. Bogayevsky. — Landscape.

133. I. Brodsky. — Winter Landscape.

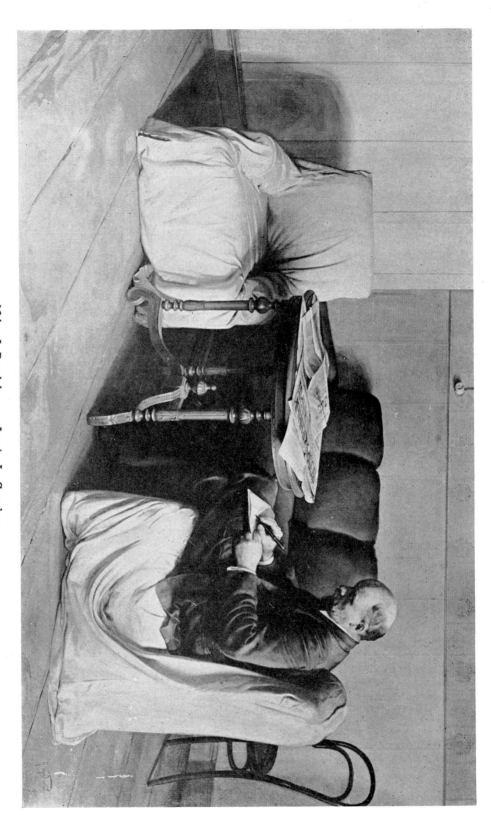

134. I. Brodsky. — Lenin In Smolny.

135. P. Korin. — Portrait Of Maxim Gorky.

136.   V. Yakovlev. — Gold Seekers Writing A Letter To The
Creator Of The Great Constitution.

137. A. Gerassimov. — In The Bath House.

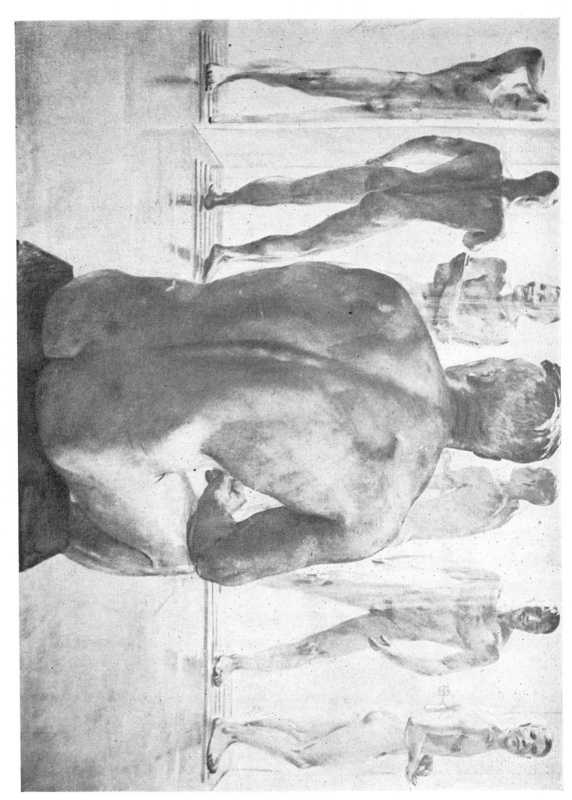

138.   A. Deineka. — Shower-Bath.

139. F. Antonov. — Love.

140. A. Samokhvalov. — Russian Girl.

141. A. Samokhvalov. — Illustration To "History Of The City"
By Saltykov-Shchedrin.

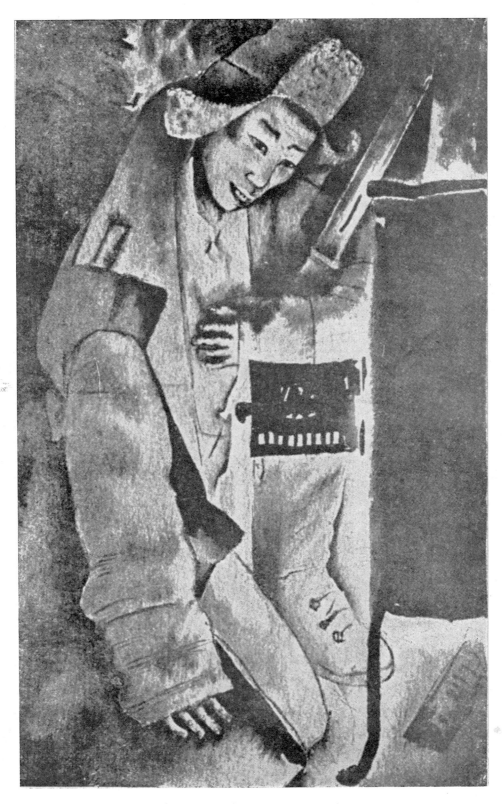

142.   A. Samokhvalov. — Khodia.

143. Kukryniksi. — Bandit Makhno.

144. M. Kurilko, Working On His Murals For The Siberian Pavillon
Of The All-Union Agricultural Fair In Moscow.

145.   M. Kurilko. — Illustration For The Fairy Tale "The Frog-Princess".

146. Ishakevitsh. Kobzar.

147.   Tatiana Marvina. — Salute To The Red Square.

148. Gaifedzhan. — Winter Landscape.

149. M. Terentyeva — (A Nanaets Woman). Nomadic Life.

150. V. Uza. — Painting A Landscape.

151. A. Mamadzhanyan. — Illustration To "David Sosunsky".

152.   A. Mamadzhanyan. — Illustration To "David Sosunsky".

153.   A. Kotukhin. — Fire-Bird.

154. Vatagin. — The Death Of Ivan Susanin.

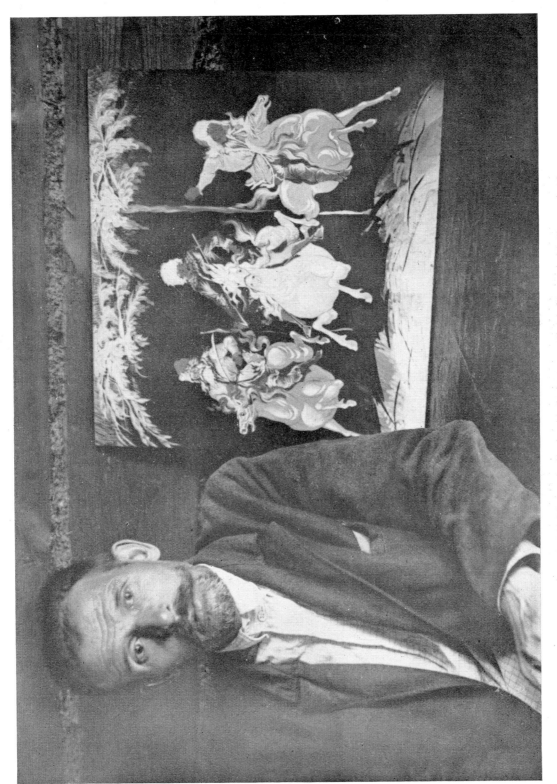

155. I. Golikov. — Red Partisans.

156.   Bakhirev. — Celebrating The Harvest At A Collective Farm.

157. Bukhara Carpet And The Weaver.

158. Sokolov-Skala, Yakovlev And Shukhmin. — Battle At Moscow.

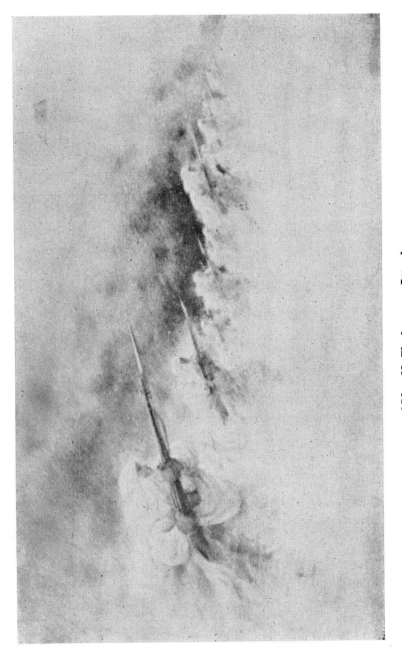

159. N. Zhukov. — Attack.

160. B. Blank. — Refugees.

161. D. Shmarinov. — Mother.

162. D. Shmarinov. — Return (From The Series "We Will Not Forget").

партизан

163.   V. Neshensky. — A Guerilla.

164. The State Tretyakov Art Gallery In Moscow.

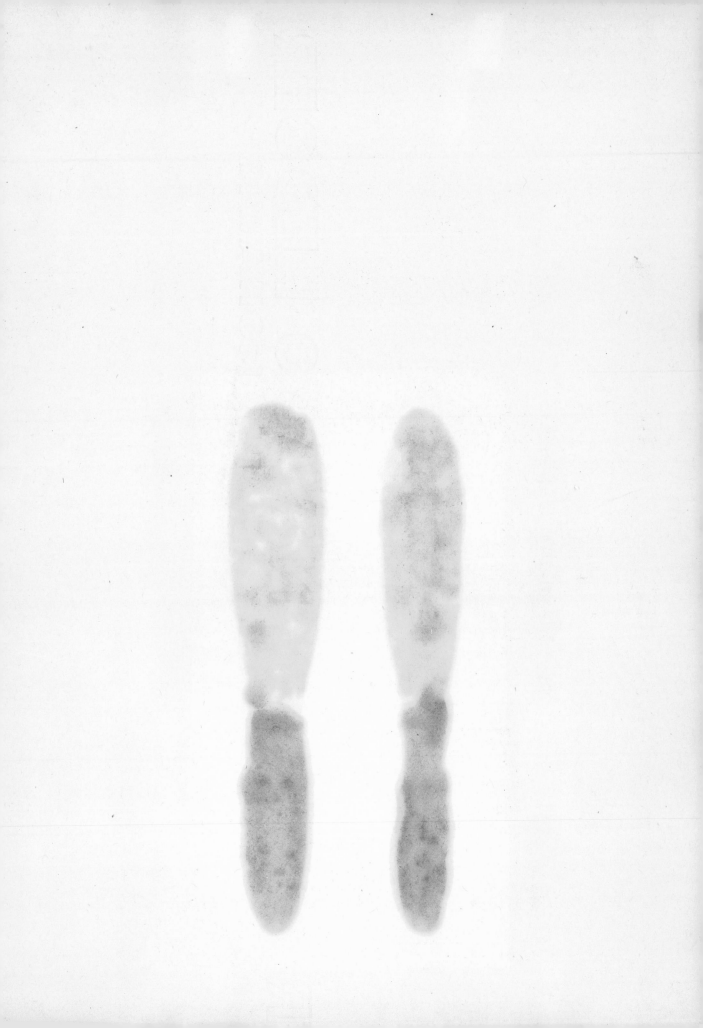

27704

ND
681
R8

RUBISSOW, HELEN
    THE ART OF RUSSIA.

DATE DUE

GAYLORD   PRINTED IN U.S.A.